Lifelines 1

Isambard Kingdom Brunel

An illustrated life of Isambard Kingdom Brunel

1806-1859

Richard Tames

Shire Publications Ltd

Engineer in exile – a silhouette of Sir Marc Isambard Brunel, father of Isambard Kingdom Brunel.

Published in 2000 by Shire Publications Ltd, Cromwell House, Church Street, Princes Risborough, Buckinghamshire HP27 9AA, UK.
Copyright © 1972 and 2000 by Richard Tames. First published 1972; reprinted 1975, 1977, 1980, 1982, 1983, 1985, 1986, 1988, 1992 and 1995. Second edition, with new text, published 2000. Number 1 in the Lifelines series. ISBN 0 7478 0459 1.
Richard Tames is hereby identified as the author of this work in accordance with Section 77 of the Copyright, Designs and Patents Act, 1988.

British Library Cataloguing in Publication Data: Tames, Richard, 1946– Isambard Kingdom Brunel; an illustrated life of Isambard Kingdom Brunel, 1806–1859. – (Lifelines; no. 1) 1. Brunel, Isambard Kingdom, 1806–1859 2. Civil engineers – Great Britain – Biography 3. Civil engineering – Great Britain – History – 19th century I. Title 624'.092 ISBN 0 7478 0459 1.

Printed in Great Britain by CIT Printing Services Ltd, Press Buildings, Merlins Bridge, Haverfordwest, Pembrokeshire SA61 1XF.

Contents

Acknowledgements

Illustrations are acknowledged as follows: Bristol City Museum and Art Gallery, pages 11, 20 (top), 26; British Rail Western Region, page 32; Brunel Society, page 31; Lady Cynthia Gladwyn, page 2; *Illustrated London News*, pages 27, 38, 42; Cadbury Lamb, pages 7, 20 (bottom), 29, 33, 43, 46; R. Lea, page 21; Museum of British Transport, Clapham, pages 4, 23, 30; Radio Times Hulton Picture Library, pages 37, 40; Science Museum, London, page 25; Smithsonian Institution, Washington, DC, page 8; Richard Tames, pages 18 (bottom), 19, 41 (bottom), 44; Reece Winstone, pages 12, 14 (both), 15 (both), 28; University of Bristol Arts Faculty Photographic Unit, page 18 (top).

Like father ...

The fame of Isambard Kingdom Brunel has all but eclipsed that of the father to whom he owed so much, both in terms of example and opportunity. Alike in their ingenuity and application, they differed strikingly in their public persona, the father unassuming and indifferent to plaudits or personal luxury, the son almost visibly ambitious and materialistic, his short stature complemented by a biting tongue and brimming self-confidence. Brunel senior was to live a decade beyond his allotted threescore years and ten, Brunel junior to find a premature grave, burned out in a blaze of glory that scorched so many others drawn to his brilliant flame.

The long life of Sir Marc Brunel (1769–1849) was a roller-coaster of adventure, adversity and adulation. He completed two major projects which have earned him an honoured place in the history of mechanical and civil engineering respectively. Even his more modest achievements – designing the Bowery Theatre in New York or transforming the efficient handling of materials in British naval dockyards – demonstrated a versatility worthy of at least an honourable footnote in any chronicle of the evolution of his profession. Further proofs of Marc Brunel's astonishing inventiveness range from novel devices for winding cotton, copying drawings and knitting textiles to processes for making ornamental tinfoil and designs for engines powered by air or gases liquefied at low temperatures – but none of them made him any money. Brunel senior's career was likewise littered with failed, abandoned or unrealised schemes – for mass-producing army boots, for a new way of printing *The Times*, for a Panama canal and for bridges over the Seine and the Neva. Marc Brunel died honoured by both his adopted country and his native land – a knight of the realm and a member of the Legion d' Honneur. Vice-President of the Royal Society, he was, however, also a graduate of the King's Bench prison for debtors.

Born at Hacqueville, near Gisors in Normandy, Marc had wilfully turned his back on a career in the church to enter the French navy as a teenager, seeing active service for six years. Ardent royalist sympathies then obliged him to flee France after the execution of Louis XVI and, upon landing in New York in 1793, to begin a new career as a surveyor and an American. Swiftly appointed chief engineer of the bustling port, Marc drew on his previous professional

---

Left: *A painting of Isambard Kingdom Brunel by his brother-in-law, the Royal Academician John Horsley. The plans on the table relate to the Thames Tunnel project.*

expertise to design for it an arsenal, a cannon foundry and a system of coastal defences.

In 1799 Marc forsook the land of opportunity to sail for England. Within the year he married Sophia Kingdom, an English girl whom he had met and fallen in love with seven years before in France. In due course he became naturalised as a Briton.

Marc was determined to persuade the Admiralty that he could revolutionise the manufacture of ships' pulley blocks, an unspectacular but crucial item of naval equipment. It took four years of lobbying to win official approval, and three more years, with the outstanding technical support of the master technician Henry Maudslay, to bring it into effect. The outcome was an integrated system of forty-three machines, which reduced the labour force required to produce a target output of 100,000 blocks a year from over one hundred skilled men to just ten semi-skilled operatives. The machinery saved the Admiralty £24,000 in the first year of operation, the year in which Isambard Kingdom Brunel was born on 9th April in Portsea, Portsmouth.

Marc Brunel's other epoch-making achievement was the successful completion of the first tunnel ever to be driven under a navigable river – a victory long deferred and eventually won only at the cost of his health. Hailed as a technical triumph, the Thames Tunnel proved a commercial catastrophe – a potent warning of similar endeavours which would punctuate the career of his son, a son who would prove equally restless, equally visionary, just as economical in technical matters and just as profligate with funds, his own as much as those of backers dazzled by his flair and energy.

As an engineer Marc Brunel had been essentially self-taught. Despite his own rejection of parental determination that he follow a clerical career, Brunel senior was determined that his son should follow his own path as an engineer and carefully devised a training to fit him for that end. Isambard never wavered from the path mapped out for him. Exhibiting a precocious talent for drawing, he eagerly learned from his paternal mentor as a small child how to execute a perfect circle freehand. A local clergyman in Chelsea introduced the boy to Latin and Greek, and then Isambard was sent to what was, by the standards of the day, a highly progressive boarding school in Hove to wrestle with Euclid's geometry and amuse himself by making model boats and drawing plans of the town. At fourteen he went to the College of Caen in his father's native Normandy to perfect his fluency in French and thus enable him to proceed to the Lycée Henri Quatre in Paris. This was a Napoleonic foundation, but Brunel senior disregarded any vestigial distaste lingering from his own royalist past, acknowledging rather the excellence of its teaching in mathematics and its role as feeder to the famed École Polytechnique, then the world's only technological university. Isambard's theoretical studies at the Lycée were complemented by a practical apprenticeship under master craftsman Louis Breguet, making and mending watches and scientific instruments. Brunel senior's confidential recommendation of the fourteen-year-old boy is revealing:

> He has now been my collaborator for several months. I have found him not only very useful but of ... unflinching perseverance. He never gets tired ... As a draughtsman he surpasses me ... He loves work.

Isambard did not disappoint Breguet and was not disappointed by him. Decades later, unwilling to accept any rival – with the sole exception of Robert Stephenson – as his professional equal, he was still proud to call himself one of Breguet's pupils.

In August 1822, along with six hundred other candidates, Isambard Brunel competed for the fewer than one hundred places annually available at the Polytechnique – but failed. He therefore returned to England to enter his father's office at 29 Poultry, London, in the shadow of the Bank of England, and continued to deepen his professional grounding by attending early morning lectures at the Royal Society and making almost daily visits to the capital's most eminent engineering works, Maudslay, Sons & Field of Lambeth.

The family business was, however, more demanding than prospering, as it was still recovering from the financial crisis which had consigned Marc to the King's Bench prison in 1821. In March 1825 Isambard, who already dreamed of great houses staffed by small armies of white-gloved servants, confided his secret resentments to his diary: 'I am most terribly pinched for money ... We keep neither carriage nor footman and only two maidservants.' By then he was busily occupied in helping his father to bid for a dock project in Bermondsey and to develop a revolutionary chemical 'gaz engine' which they both hoped would make them a fortune. While the engine was eventually to be abandoned

Brunel's childhood home on the river front at Chelsea.

7

Sir Marc Brunel's tunnelling-shield, inspired by his observation of the ship-worm, began work on the Thames Tunnel in 1825. Skilled excavators stood stacked in individual cubicles, edging the shield forward (to the right in this picture) while bricklayers shored up behind them and labourers carried out spoil.

after a decade of effort and expense, in the very month that the engineering tiro despaired of fame and fortune work began on the project that was to launch him as a professional in his own right.

Building a tunnel under the river Thames had first been suggested in 1798 and attempted in 1805, only to end in near disaster. The original engineer, Robert Vazie, having exhausted the initial capital of the Thames Archway Company to almost no effect, the project had been handed over to the famed Richard Trevithick. Working with a picked team of fellow Cornishmen, he overcame the treacherous quicksands that had defeated Vazie and in six months drove 1000 feet (305 metres) of tunnel – five-sixths of the required length – only to have his work destroyed in January 1808 by an abnormally high tide which totally overwhelmed his pumps.

Marc Brunel addressed the challenge armed with his newly invented tunnelling-shield, which had been inspired by his observations of destructive shipworms boring relentlessly through timber in Chatham dockyard. Having sunk a shaft 50 feet (15 metres) across and 40 feet (12 metres) deep some three-quarters of a mile (1.2 km) west of Trevithick's abortive effort, on 28th November 1825 Marc ordered the huge cast-iron device to begin edging forward under the river. Work at the face was handled by a picked élite of Durham miners while Irish labourers carried out the spoil. The geologist's promise of solid clay soon proved false as irruptions of sewage-laden water brought progress to a crawl. Working conditions at the face were hazardous in the extreme, the vile stench of foul air reducing exhausted navvies to total collapse and a mysterious

8

'tunnel sickness' inflicting upon them terrifying afflictions, ranging from rotting fingernails to total and permanent blindness. The resident engineer, William Armstrong, cracked under the strain. Isambard, just twenty, took his place but received neither his title nor a commensurate salary until January 1827. Cat-napping in the tunnel itself and frequently staying underground for three twelve-hour shifts at a stretch, he revelled in the work, despite the additional irritation of shilling sightseers who came to see engineering history being made. Marc, who had vehemently opposed this fund-raising gimmick, meanwhile brooded on the possibility of a cave-in drowning not only his son and workforce but dozens of visitors as well.

Catastrophe struck at high water on 18th May 1827 as leakages became uncontrollable and a tidal wave carried all before it through the tunnel. Isambard got his crew half-way up the shaft before the lower section of the stairway down was demolished. On reaching safety, he heard a faint cry from below and at once descended to tie a rope round a half-conscious navvy. Not a single man had been lost. Isambard inspected the damage from a diving bell the following day, disregarding the local curate's thunderous warning of 'a just judgement on the presumptuous aspirations of mortal men'. It took six months to clear the wreckage. Isambard celebrated with a banquet for fifty select guests in the gas-lit reclaimed workings, flamboyantly embellished with crimson draperies. In the background 120 élite miners scoffed beef and beer while the band of the Coldstream Guards provided a stirring musical accompaniment.

Celebration was, however, premature. On 12th January 1828 water once more overwhelmed the shield. Isambard was saved by the very force of the tidal wave, which, having knocked him senseless and carried him the length of the tunnel, bore him up a shaft, whence he was snatched to safety. Seconds later, the receding wave would have dragged him down to join the six men lost in the calamity. Afterwards he noted with bravado that 'the sight and whole affair was well worth the risk and I would willingly pay my share ... of the expenses of such a "spectacle".' Perhaps, but the debacle cost him a broken leg. He chafed at the thought that, a generation before, William Pitt had been Prime Minister in his twenties and, while he currently endured months of enforced idleness, his near contemporaries, the Scots John and George Rennie, had won the contract to rebuild London Bridge. When work on the Thames Tunnel did finally resume seven years later, Isambard would be too busily engaged on far greater schemes to lend a hand again. But, before that, a period of chastening was to be endured – 'unemployed' and, worse still, 'untalked-of'.

A mediocre success

Convalescence gave Brunel the opportunity to dream – of outbuilding the Rennies' London Bridge with a spectacular 300 foot (91 metre) span, or of driving another tunnel under the Thames at Gravesend and 'at last be rich, have a house built, of which I have even made the *drawings* etc., be the first engineer and an example for future ones'. That his track record so far consisted of an abandoned tunnel faced him with the real possibility of failure in his chosen profession. An even worse nightmare was for him to become 'a mediocre success … sometimes employed, sometimes not – £200 or £300 a year and that uncertain'.

Persisting with the 'gaz engine' experiments in case it might still prove successful, Brunel, with the help of his father and friends, gained a series of humdrum commissions – drainage works on the Essex coast at Tollesbury; a new dock at Monkwearmouth, Sunderland; surveys of canals and bridges – all of which kept him on the move and afforded incidental opportunities to examine sites and buildings throughout Britain. Encouragement must also have come from his election as a Fellow of the Royal Society at the very early age of twenty-four. Nor did he cease to dream. Riding on the newly opened Liverpool & Manchester Railway, he wrote prophetically: 'I record this specimen of the shaking of the Manchester Railway. The time is not far off when we shall be able to take our coffee and write while going noiselessly and smoothly at 45 mph – let me try.' Real life, however, continued to douche the dreams. Work on Monkwearmouth was suspended indefinitely. Plans were shelved for a dry dock at Woolwich, on which he had lavished hours in making surveys and site trials. And the minor social triumph of building an observatory at Kensington for the eminent astronomer Sir James South was marred by an unseemly squabble over the payment of a typically Brunellian cost overrun. Further possibilities of prestigious employment in the provinces evaporated when he was turned down for the post of engineer with the Newcastle & Carlisle Railway and the Bristol & Birmingham Railway.

It was while convalescing in Bristol after the tunnel cave-in that Brunel had learned of the local proposal to throw a bridge across the Avon Gorge at Clifton. When a competition for designs was opened he gave the organisers a choice of four sites, with detailed plans for each. On this occasion, however, it was the father who was to put in long days assisting the son in preparing the submission. Acting as final arbiter, Thomas Telford, first President of the Institution

This drawing by Brunel, dated 1831, was probably one of the designs which he submitted to the second competition for the Clifton Bridge. A similar sketch, showing the Egyptian-style decoration which was finally adopted, has not survived.

of Civil Engineers and doyen of the profession, rejected every single competition entry and, when requested to do so by the embarrassed organisers, submitted his own proposal – subsequently characterised as the 'one truly monstrous aberration of his long career'. A second competition was announced. Brunel won it. But once again success was dashed from his grasp by fate, this time in the form of three days of rioting and arson throughout Bristol following rejection by the House of Lords of a Parliamentary Reform Bill. Brunel, though personally sympathetic to reform, was even more sympathetic to public order and the sanctity of property and therefore enrolled as a special constable and even attempted, manfully but ultimately unsuccessfully, to arrest a looter by main force. Armed with the back of a broken chair, he helped salvage corporation plate from the ravaged Mansion House and later gave evidence at the trial of the luckless mayor. First-hand experience of mob violence did not, however, dissuade Brunel from later campaigning for his brother-in-law Benjamin Hawes when he stood successfully for Lambeth as a Radical in the first election after the passage of the 1832 Reform Act. The supposedly Radical Hawes subsequently went on to become a notoriously conservative War Office bureaucrat but the ties of

This photograph of Brunel was probably taken in the 1850s.

family ensured that he remained one of Brunel's closest friends.

Devastated Bristol postponed the bridge scheme until 1835. Further difficulties delayed completion until 1864, five years after Brunel's death. For once, however, the effort had not been entirely wasted. Local contacts made in the course of the bridge venture secured Brunel a commission to devise a drag-boat system for scouring the docks of silt. That work in turn brought him into contact with a consortium looking for a surveyor to plan a railway route from Bristol to London, the greatest single such undertaking yet contemplated. Brunel promised them not the cheapest route but the best. Almost despite this bravura gesture, he got the job – by a single vote. It was the turning-point of his career.

For ten weeks Brunel rode ceaselessly to and fro along his chosen line of route, covering up to 40 miles (64 km) a day, measuring ground levels and gradients and enthusing local landowners with the advantages that would accrue to them by allowing the line to pass over their property. Even he confessed that 'it is harder work than I like. I am rarely much under 20 hours a day at it.' On 30th July 1832 he made a first public presentation of his plans, estimating the budget, including stations and locomotives, at a stupendous £2,500,000. It would eventually cost more than twice as much.

On the strength of the survey Isambard was confirmed as Engineer of the proposed Great Western Railway on 7th March 1833. On the strength of the appointment he took out a loan to rent a drawing office at 53 Parliament Street, minutes from the House of Commons. Henceforth he would leave behind the days of travelling on hired hacks or freezing on a stage-coach as an 'outside' passenger. Instead he had a four-horse britschka built to his own design, incorporating a fold-away bed and drawing-board, storage for surveying gear and a box for fifty cigars. Navvies nicknamed it the 'Flying Hearse'.

The Bill to authorise the GWR went to its Commons Committee stage on 16th April 1834 with Brunel serving as its main proponent. Badgered by hostile counsel, he remained masterly in his command of detail and of his own propensities for temper and sarcasm – only to have the Bill later thrown out by the Lords. Revised proposals were submitted in 1835, Brunel personally enduring no less than eleven days of cross-examination. An eyewitness described his performance as 'an intellectual treat'. Brunel shrugged off any suggestion of self-doubt in the face of formidably foxy lawyers on the simple grounds that they 'could not possibly know as much about engineering as I'. By the time the Bill was finally approved the demonic engineer was already in the thick of marking out subsidiary routes linking in towns and cities from Oxford down to

The Clifton Suspension Bridge, Bristol, designed by Isambard Brunel. *Above left: An 1836 print of the design which won the competition, showing sphinxes on top of the towers. Above right: Construction was abandoned in the 1830s and not resumed until 1861, after Brunel had died. The two towers on either side of*

the Avon Gorge became known as the 'Follies'. Below left: *The two sides of the road about to meet as the bridge nears completion in 1864.* Below right: *Clifton Bridge as it is today. The bridge is 230 feet (70 metres) above high water, has a span of 630 feet (192 metres) and weighs 7000 tons.*

Plymouth and westwards into south Wales which would make the GWR the strategic spine of a regional railway empire.

On Boxing Night 1835 Brunel sat alone in his Parliament Street office to set down his thoughts in the diary he had scarcely touched in two frantic years:

> What a blank in my journal! And during the most eventful part in my life. When I last wrote in this book I was just emerging from obscurity. I had been toiling most unprofitably at numerous things ... what a change. *The Railway* is now in progress ... the finest work in England – a handsome salary – £2,000 a year – on excellent terms with my Directors and all going smoothly, but what a fight we have had – and how near defeat – and what a ruinous defeat it would have been ... And it's not this alone but everything I have been engaged in has been successful. *Clifton Bridge* – my first child, my darling, is actually going – recommenced last Monday – Glorious! *Sunderland Docks* too going well. *Bristol Docks* all Bristol is alive and turned bold and speculative with this Railway – we are to widen the entrances and the Lord knows what.

The roster of projects continued with four branch lines, plus a suspension bridge across the Thames and, as an afterthought, 'I forgot also Bristol and Gloster Railway'. Brunel reckoned the capital involved in these enterprises to surpass £5,300,000, then forsook his preening to ponder – 'it can't last ... Let me see the storm in time to gather in my sails.'

It is an exceptional man who manages to balance devotion to work and family. Marc Brunel was one such but his son was not. Assured at last of professional eminence, Brunel junior determined that 'this time 12 months I shall be a married man'. Mary Horsley, whose family he had known for five years, was qualified by her beauty and elegance to preside over the stylish sort of household he had set his mind on and she accepted her role with alacrity. Brunel snatched time from his crowded schedule to be married by special licence in Kensington parish church on 5th July 1836. Their honeymoon consisted of a frantic fortnight in a jolting coach, crisscrossing the country to follow an itinerary that paid as much attention to sites as sights. The newlyweds then settled above yet another new drawing office at 18 Duke Street. They might be living 'over the shop' but the shop *was* in St James's.

God's Wonderful Railway

When Brunel began working on the Great Western Railway he was not yet thirty, had never built a railway before and had no trained assistants. Forging a great north–south link via Birmingham was absorbing the talents of the foremost existing contractors and foremen. Brunel was therefore faced with the dual challenge of supervising the most ambitious single construction project in British history and simultaneously welding a scratch workforce into a disciplined team. The Thames Tunnel experience showed that he could lead from the front, sharing all discomforts and braving all dangers. Fortunately another of Brunel's qualities was a talent for picking talent. One of his assistants, Charles Richardson, went on to build the Severn Tunnel and to invent the cane-spliced cricket bat. Another, William Froude, became the world's leading expert on modelling ships to test the design of their construction. Brunel expected his senior colleagues to be gentlemen in their exercise of authority and his juniors to be diligent in the performance of their duties. If he could charm a duke whose land he needed to cross or sack a workman on the spot for drunkenness or insubordination, Brunel could also excoriate his technical staff for shortcomings with withering venom, as in a letter to a draughtsman who constantly vexed him by making drawings on the back of others:

> You are a cursed, lazy, inattentive, apathetic vagabond, and if you continue to neglect my instructions, and to show such infernal laziness, I shall send you about your business ... you have again wasted more of my time than your whole life is worth, in looking for the altered drawings ... they won't do!

Resolute to realise his ideal of high-speed luxury travel for the coffee-drinking, journal-keeping classes, Brunel had surveyed a route unparalleled for the infrequency and gradualness of its gradients. In pioneering railways just a decade before George Stephenson had fixed on the gauge for his track – 4 feet $8^1/2$ inches (1435 mm) – by the simple expedient of taking the average of the coal carts traditionally used on his native Tyneside. Almost without question this had become the 'standard gauge'. Brunel scorned such pragmatism and sought, by calculation and experiment, to derive from first principles the gauge best suited to speed and smoothness of operation. The result was a 'broad gauge' of 7 feet (2143 mm), capable, he argued, of accommodating larger carriages, travelling closer to the ground and therefore, when driven by larger engines, better able to reconcile speed with stability. Broad gauge certainly

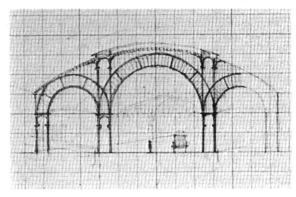

From Brunel's sketchbooks in Bristol University Library, this is a drawing for Paddington station.

suited the Bristol–London route – the flattest main line in Britain – but its adoption increased the cost of constructing larger curves, points and earthworks and raised a further major difficulty: how to manage through traffic from systems using standard gauge. This amounted, as Michael Robbins has observed, to 'a failure not of technique but of administrative imagination'. Nevertheless, it was to enable the GWR to inaugurate the world's first express train service, running between Paddington and Exeter in just four hours forty minutes.

While the engineering profession fiercely debated the pros and cons of 'the battle of the gauges', Brunel immersed himself in myriads of detail as construction of the GWR pressed ahead. Knowledge of local rainfall figures was a precondition for calculating how to stabilise earthworks and budget the time for their construction. Even time itself had to be calculated. Greenwich Mean Time was not to be adopted for almost another half

A memorial plaque at Paddington station depicts Brunel smoking the inevitable cigar.

18

century, so stations usually displayed two clocks, one showing the actual local time, the other London-based 'railway time', the variation between the two amounting to fifteen minutes by the time Bristol was reached. And there still remained the semi-permanent vexation of having to resort periodically to Parliament for further enabling legislation. In June 1837 Brunel reported furiously to the directors of the GWR:

> A new delay has occurred in the progress of our Bills – a new Crotchet has come across some Lord's head and a new Clause is sent to the Commons for approval – this utter wanton disregard of the interests of the parties waiting is really disgusting. The Tyranny exercised is as great as it could be under the most despotic Government and the only answer that one gets to the strongest appeals is insult and ridicule. If I had not been a Radical before, I should become one now.

As work proceeded Brunel's perfectionism cast him into a state of constant anxiety. He confided to a friend how he was haunted by 'a little swarm of devils in the shape of leaky tanks, uncut timber, half-finished station houses, sinking embankments, broken screws, absent guard plates, unfinished drawings...'. At least he found a reliable, if touchy, genius in the locomotive department, twenty-one-year-old Daniel Gooch, who noted rather unsympathetically in his *Memoirs* almost half a century later: 'One feature of Brunel's character ... that gave him a great deal of extra and unnecessary work, was that he fancied that no one could do anything but himself.'

Collaboration was not entirely eschewed. Much of the architectural detailing at Paddington was sub-contracted to Matthew Digby Wyatt and the ornamentation to the designer Owen

A loyal supporter – the sign of the Daniel Gooch pub at Paddington.

This lithograph of the interior of Bristol station (Temple Meads) was one of a series by J. C. Bourne published in 1842 and showing the GWR in its original form. Trains first ran from Bristol to Bath on 31st August 1840, and to London on 30th June 1841. Note the broad-gauge locomotive and rolling stock. The pseudo-medieval hammerbeam roof-span impressed contemporaries.

Jones. The station hotel was the work of Philip Hardwick. The Great Western Hotel at Bristol was conceived in general terms by Brunel but designed in detail by a local architect, R. S. Pope. Temple Meads station in Bristol, however, was substantially Brunel's own creation, an exercise in the newly fashionable Gothic taste. Augustus Pugin,

doyen of Gothic revivalists, dismissed it as 'engineer's architecture ... at once costly and offensive and full of pretension'. Travellers were, however, impressed by the immense span of its hammerbeam roof. Brunel's taste for the Gothic also emerged along the route itself where he left one tunnel mouth deliberately incomplete so that it might resemble a ruinous medieval gateway; he even had ivy trained over it to enhance the picturesque effect.

Temple Meads station, Bristol.

Brunel's brick bridge taking the Great Western Railway over the Thames at Maidenhead.

To aid its cash-flow, the GWR was opened to traffic in sections, as soon as they were completed. The first, from London to Taplow, near Maidenhead, was opened on 4th June 1838. Early traffic, however, experienced a bumpy ride and a couple of derailments. At the half-yearly company meeting held in August 1838 critics successfully moved for a progress report by consulting engineers. Brunel, ably supported by Gooch, inaugurated a series of trials to disprove their contention that poor performance at high speed was caused by wind resistance to the increased frontal area of broad-gauge engines. The real problem was shown to be a constricted blast-pipe which throttled the engine as it accelerated. Once altered, the engines showed that they could not only pull heavy trains at more than 40 mph (64 km/h) but also do so on less fuel than previously thought possible.

Vanquishing human opposition, Brunel turned to do battle with the elements. Torrential rains drowned the Thames valley in the autumn of 1839, reducing the 2 mile (3.2 km) Sonning Cutting to a quagmire. Brunel took personal charge of the twelve hundred navvies and two hundred horses engaged on the work and completed it by the year's end. By March 1840 the line was open as far as Reading, its smoothness convincingly demonstrated by Gooch's *Firefly*, which averaged 50 mph (80 km/h) on a 30 mile (48 km) run.

Work from the Bristol end went much more slowly, involving a

The west front of Box Tunnel, drawn by Bourne. Nearly 2 miles (3 km) long, far greater than any previous tunnel, Box cost the lives of more than a hundred men.

series of major engineering problems. The stations at both Bristol and Bath had to be elevated above ground level and the latter approached by a viaduct of seventy-three arches. Between the two stations another viaduct of twenty-eight arches, four major bridges and seven tunnels were needed. By May 1841, however, only the Chippenham–Bath section remained unfinished, but the route included a crossing of the Avon, two viaducts, diverting the Kennet & Avon Canal and driving the greatest tunnel ever attempted. Building Box Tunnel can fairly be described as a bloody business, costing over a hundred lives. Almost 2 miles (3.2 km) long, it absorbed a ton of gunpowder, a ton of candles and the labour of four thousand men every week for thirty months, while a hundred carts were employed to bring in thirty million bricks. In December 1840, when it was four months overdue, Brunel once again took personal charge. The huge quantities of stone extracted as spoil yielded building materials for neat cottages to house the labour force in the 'Railway Village' adjacent to the locomotive works at Swindon.

The entire route was finally opened in June 1841. It had cost £6,500,000, more than double the original estimate, but it was, indeed, 'the finest work in England'. The ultimate contemporary accolade was conveyed when, on 13th June 1842, Queen Victoria chose to

An early picture of Slough (for Windsor) station and the Royal Hotel. Queen Victoria took her first train ride from here in 1842.

make her first ever journey by rail on the GWR, travelling from Slough into London with Brunel and Gooch riding the locomotive footplate. Time has only enhanced the verdict of Brunel's own day. As that doyen of industrial historians, Anthony Burton, has observed, 'a century and a half after work began, the mere mention of the initials GWR will bring the enthusiasts scampering. Many transport systems have been admired: the GWR was, and is, loved.'

Ruling the waves

Construction work on the Great Western Railway had scarcely begun when Brunel simultaneously threw himself into yet another novel challenge. In October 1835 a GWR director complained that the line was too long ever to be completed. Brunel responded that, on the contrary, it should stretch all the way to New York by linking in with a dedicated steamship service. The result of this typically Brunellian outburst, at once spontaneous, flamboyant and prescient, was the formation of a separate Great Western Steamship Company and the construction of the *Great Western*. But whereas the GWR was entirely the personal creation of the highly paid I. K. Brunel, Chief Engineer, the *Great Western* project was to be a collaborative venture, drawing on the expertise of a team, albeit inspired and co-ordinated by Brunel's drive and unremunerated services.

Marc Brunel, a former naval officer, had been involved in several steamship ventures and patented improvements to the design of both engines and paddles, though his schemes for a London–Margate steamer service and a fleet of steam tugs for towing Royal Navy vessels had both come to nothing. Marc, like most of his generation, believed that 'steam cannot do for distant navigation' because no steamer could possibly carry enough fuel for an ocean crossing. The proper role of steam on the high seas was to serve as an auxiliary power source, moving ships becalmed or allowing them to fight contrary winds and currents. Steamers pure and simple seemed destined to serve as ferries or coasters, valued for their regularity and reliability but confined to the high-value carriage of passengers and mails rather than the transportation of bulky goods over great distances.

Isambard Brunel, however, believed that the answer was simply to build larger ships. Marc's generation assumed that doubling the size of a hull would mean doubling the power needed to move it. Isambard spotted the fallacy behind this reasoning and formulated what became a fundamental rule of naval architecture – that whereas the carrying capacity of a hull increases as the *cube* of its dimensions, its resistance (the power needed to drive it through water) increases only as the *square* of those dimensions. It all boiled down to the distinction between increasing volume and increasing surface area and, once stated, seemed unbelievably simple and obvious.

Construction of the *Great Western* began in July 1836. Built of oak by traditional methods, it embodied no major technical innovations but was distinguished by an immensely strong hull, designed to withstand the worst of storms. Displacing 2300 tons, the *Great Western*

A model of the 'Great Western', Brunel's first steamship, which made her first Atlantic crossing in fifteen days in 1838.

was 236 feet (71.9 metres) long and 35 feet (10.7 metres) broad. London and Liverpool at once took up Bristol's challenge, laying down the *British Queen* and *Liverpool* respectively to stake their claim to a share of the New York route. When it became clear that the *Great Western* would be ready long before her rivals the London consortium chartered the 703 ton *Sirius* to stand in for their ship. On 28th March 1838 she left the Thames to fuel her newly enlarged bunkers at Cork, before attempting the first all-steam crossing of the Atlantic. A flurry of final tests enabled the *Great Western* to set out in pursuit just three days later.

Disaster struck her early next day when the *Great Western*'s boiler lagging caught fire, filling the engine-room with smoke and igniting the underside of the decks. Brunel, in his haste to assist, fell nearly 20 feet (6 metres) from a half-burnt ladder, his fall into the water on the engine-room floor being broken by a seaman, who pulled him clear of danger. Brunel was evacuated to convalesce on Canvey Island and it was not until 8th April that the *Great Western* finally left Bristol.

The *Sirius*, a day nearer its destination, had started on 4th April. Contrary winds tested her resolution but after nineteen days at sea she reached New York with barely 15 tons of coal in her bunkers. Welcomed as heroes, her crew were almost immediately upstaged by the sudden arrival of the *Great Western*, fifteen days out of Bristol and with 200 tons of coal to spare. *Sirius* had won the race by bold seamanship but the *Great Western*, overhauling her by a steady two knots, pointed to a future in which steam navigation would become a matter of commercial routine rather than heroic endeavour. The *Great Western* would become the world's first regular transatlantic steamer and over the following eight years would make sixty-seven

A hand-coloured lithograph, published by George Davey & Son, showing the 'Great Britain' being floated out of the Great Western dry dock, Bristol, on 19th July 1843.

The 'Great Britain' was originally built with six masts but after it had made four transatlantic crossings extensive alterations were made. This engraving from the 'Illustrated London News' shows the refitted ship with five masts.

crossings, including one eastbound run of twelve days six hours. Later she was transferred to the West Indies mail run before being finally broken up at Vauxhall on the Thames in 1857.

Even before the *Great Western* had finished her second voyage Brunel was already planning her successor, this time incorporating major innovations in style, structure, materials and propulsion. The *Great Britain* was to be of iron, with a screw propeller rather than paddles and with engines capable of delivering 1500 horsepower to achieve a speed of 12 knots, although she was also fitted with six masts so that sail could be used as a back-up. At 3270 gross tons and 332 feet (101 metres) in length, she was of unprecedented size and was also the first ship to be constructed with watertight bulkheads. Construction began in 1839. In 1843 she was launched by the Prince Consort after the lock chambers of Bristol Dock had been partly demolished to enable her great bulk to squeeze through at high tide, an operation accomplished with only inches and minutes to spare. Fitting out took until the summer of 1845, but all went smoothly on the maiden voyage, when she carried sixty first class passengers, as well as steerage passengers and 600 tons of cargo.

On 22nd September 1846 the *Great Britain* left Liverpool for her fifth crossing with a record complement of 180 passengers. Hours later she ran aground in darkness on the coast of County Down, not, as the captain thought, of the Isle of Man. (The unprecedented amount of iron in the hull had affected the ship's compass.) Panic ensued but no lives were lost. A wooden vessel would have broken up in the circumstances but the immense strength of the *Great Britain* saved her not only from the initial shock but also from a subsequent winter-long battering of gales. When salvage experts failed to refloat the holed vessel Brunel came to her rescue. Exasperated that what he modestly called 'the finest ship in the world' should be left 'lying, like a useless saucepan kicking about on the most exposed shore you can imagine', he organised its protection with 'a mass of large, strong faggots lashed together, skewered together with iron rods, weighted down with iron, sandbags etc., wrapping the whole round with chains, just like a huge poultice'.

Successfully reclaimed in the spring of 1847, the *Great Britain*, having bankrupted the Great Western Steamship Company, was sold in 1850 to Gibbs, Bright & Company and redirected to the Australia run, carrying an average six hundred emigrants on the outward voyage and bullion on the return. During the Crimean War (1854–6) and the Indian Rebellion (1857) she was pressed into service as a troopship. After twenty-three years on the Australia run the *Great Britain* was laid up in 1875 and remodelled in 1882 as a sailing ship, her iron hull sheathed in wood. During a disastrous voyage to Panama she was battered and dismasted by a terrific

The 'Great Britain' returning to her birthplace dock at Bristol on 19th July 1970. On board were HRH the Duke of Edinburgh and Mr Jack Hayward, who gave £150,000 for the ship's salvage.

*The restored SS
'Great Britain' is
open to the public
in the Great
Western Dock in
Bristol, where she
was built in 1839–
43.*

gale before finding refuge in the Falkland Islands. Condemned as unseaworthy, in 1886 she was bought and used as a storage hulk for wood and coal until 1937, when, judged incapable of even this ignoble duty, she was beached in Sparrow Cove to rot. She was finally rescued in 1970. The *Great Britain* returned to her birthplace dock on 19th July that year, carrying HRH the Duke of Edinburgh and Mr Jack Hayward, who had given £150,000 towards the salvage costs. The *Great Britain* has since been lovingly restored and, alone of Brunel's three great ships, survives as testimony to his vision and enterprise.

Back on the rails

As Brunel had envisaged, the Great Western Railway sprouted branches reaching out to other western cities. When the broad gauge met its rival at Gloucester Parliament appointed a Royal Commission to investigate the problems this raised. Brunel proposed to demonstrate the superiority of his specification by means of speed trials, a sporting gesture considering that a new generation of improved locomotives had only recently been introduced on the narrower gauge. In December 1845 Gooch's Firefly class locomotive *Ixion* made three round trips of 106 miles (171 km) from Paddington to Didcot hauling loads of 60, 70 and 80 tons, averaging 50 mph (80 km/h) with 60 tons and touching 60 mph (97 km/h) with 80 tons.

The break of gauge at Gloucester. Despite the superior performance of Brunel's broad-gauge trains, Parliament declared the 4 feet 8¹/₂ inch (1435 mm) gauge to be standard and the GWR had to change. This impression of frantic bustle and anxiety contrasts strongly with the ordered elegance depicted on page 23.

Brunel's northern rivals, running the 88 miles (142 km) from York to Darlington and back, achieved a best of 53 mph (85 km/h) with a 50 ton load. The Gauge Commissioners, however, took the view that speed was not the sole criterion. More to the point was the fact that it was much easier and cheaper to narrow a railway than widen it, and the 274 miles (441 km) of broad gauge in operation scarcely compared with the 1900 miles (3058 km) built to the narrower gauge – which henceforth was officially deemed to be 'standard'. The GWR was therefore obliged to lay a third intermediate rail for the benefit of standard rolling-stock. Pamphlet warfare sustained

Old atmospheric railway tubes photographed about 1911 at Paignton, in use as surface water drains.

'the battle of the gauges' intermittently for a while, and Brunel toyed with the idea of a form of containerisation to cut down the labour and expense of transhipment from one gauge to the other; but the Commissioners' definitive decision effectively confined the broad gauge to its existing territory, although it was not finally abandoned there until 1892.

In 1845 Britain was in the grip of such a 'railway mania' that it appalled even Brunel's free-market instincts, as he made clear to a correspondent in France:

> I am really sick of hearing proposals made. I wish it were at an end. I prefer engineering very much to projecting, of which I keep as clear as I can ... I wish I could suggest a plan that would greatly diminish the number of projects; it would suit my interests and those of my clients perfectly if all railways were stopped for several years to come.

Brunel's persistent experiments with the 'gaz' engine stand as evidence of his interest in the idea of a power source that might be both smokeless and virtually silent. When the brothers Samuda demonstrated the possibilities of an 'atmospheric railway' on a $1^1/4$ mile (2 km) stretch of abandoned roadbed on the Birmingham, Bristol & Thames Junction Railway, Brunel sensed something promising, despite Stephenson's dismissal of it as 'a great humbug'. In 1843 a slightly longer line was opened from Kingstown, Dublin, to Dalkey, and crowds rushed to glide at 30 mph (48 km/h) on the apparent marvel. Its basic propulsion technology was simple – a pipe, laid between tracks, within which a piston ran, joined to a carriage above via a flanged groove along the top of the pipe. Steam pumps at intervals along the track extracted air from in front of the train, creating a partial vacuum and thus causing the piston to be moved forward by the atmospheric pressure behind it. It was simply magnificent and magnificently simple. It impressed observers from the Board of Trade and the French Public Works Department. It

The atmospheric railway pumping house at Totnes in 1911. It was never used for its intended purpose.

impressed Brunel, who therefore ordered the installation of an atmospheric system along a sizeable section of the South Devon Railway, for which he had become responsible. As on other occasions, however, he failed to reckon with technical limitations, which frustrated the translation of elegant theory into brute practice. For a few months in 1847–8 a regular atmospheric railway service did operate between Exeter and Newton Abbot, attaining impressive *average* speeds of 64 mph (103 km/h), despite problems of air leakage and faulty pumping engines. Brunel assured himself that if he installed electric telegraphs in the pumping houses he could vastly increase their efficiency by synchronising their efforts more closely. Time revealed, however, much more basic defects and shortcomings. Many of the slotted pipes had been inaccurately cast. The leather flange froze stiff as a board or was eaten by rats and by June 1848 was disintegrating along its entire length. Replacing that alone would have cost £25,000. Brunel therefore abruptly called off the whole venture, one of the most costly failures in the history of engineering to that date. The sale of the pumping machinery alone fetched £40,000.

If the atmospheric railway was a costly fiasco, the Royal Albert Bridge at Saltash proved a spectacular success. As the broad gauge

The Royal Albert Bridge across the Tamar at Saltash was opened in 1859. It was more than a century before the parallel road bridge was opened in 1961.

thrust west from Plymouth it had to cross the Tamar, the ancient boundary between Devon and Cornwall. At the chosen crossing point the river was 1100 feet (335 metres) wide and 70 feet (21 metres) deep. Brunel opted for two spans of 465 feet (142 metres), each weighing 1000 tons, to be supported by a single masonry column, which would be built inside a cast-iron coffer dam. Begun in June 1854, the supporting pier was completed by the end of 1856. But the assembly of the first truss and the complex arrangement of pontoons and pulleys required to position it correctly took longer, and it was not until 1st September 1857 that Brunel could attempt to direct the monumental task of jacking it into position. Directing his men by means of flags and numbers, the diminutive engineer proceeded under the gaze of an awe-struck crowd of thousands. 'Not a voice was heard', wrote an eyewitness, 'as by some mysterious agency, the tube and rail ... travelled to their resting place ... With the impressive silence which is the highest evidence of power, it slid, as it were, into its position.... .' The tension broke. A Marine band launched into 'See, the conquering hero comes', and Brunel, free at last to relish the theatricality of the occasion, acknowledged the ovation of the onlookers. The second span at Saltash was floated in July 1858, and the bridge was formally opened by the Prince Consort in May 1859.

Public and private

Brunel could scarcely be described as a political being, at least in the party sense, and he persistently rebutted attempts to persuade him to stand for Parliament. By instinct he was a free marketeer, opposed to government regulation and regarding even the patent laws as restrictive of enterprise. Engineering problems he thought best sorted out by engineers rather than bureaucrats, noting 'With fear and regret ... this tendency to legislate and to rule, which is the fashion of the day' on the grounds that it could only 'shackle the progress of improvement tomorrow by recording and registering as law the prejudices and errors of today'. This might be interpreted as either a naive faith in the integrity of professional men or an unreasonable suspicion of the servants of the state. But Brunel was living through a period when professional men, through newly founded institutions, were striving strenuously to set themselves ever higher standards of performance and behaviour. (Brunel at times spoke as though high business standards followed automatically from gentlemanly status.) And at the same time the apparatus of government was still staffed predominantly by the nominees of the political in-crowd, their sole qualification for office being the recommendation of an influential relative or friend. Charles Dickens satirised the breed mercilessly in *Little Dorrit* in his sketch of the cumbrous and costly workings of the Circumlocution Office.

But if Brunel was by no means drawn to the world of politics, he did like to hobnob with people of influence and acknowledged their value. He willingly gave evidence to a number of official commissions on railways and, indeed, might have felt it a slight upon his standing had he not been asked to do so. Considering the rather dismal experiences his father had had in extracting promised funds from the Royal Navy for numerous projects, it is perhaps surprising that in 1841 Brunel agreed to conduct a series of trials which by 1845 had finally convinced the Admiralty of the value of the screw propeller – no mean achievement.

Having served as a volunteer to preserve order in Bristol in 1830, Brunel enrolled again as a special constable during the Chartist tensions of 1848. In 1850 he received the more exalted invitation to support Prince Albert's project for a 'Great Exhibition of the Works of Industry of All Nations'. In the same year he was also elected Vice President of the Institution of Civil Engineers. Appropriately Brunel served as a member both of the building committee of the Great Exhibition and as chairman and reporter of the section on civil engineering.

Public eminence allied with personal wealth encouraged Brunel in the lifestyle to which he had always aspired. The apartments at 18 Duke Street were extended to run above Number 17 as well, and the census of 1851 shows that to care for himself, his wife and three children Brunel employed no less than eleven servants. Brunel sent both his sons to Harrow rather than subjecting them to the sort of rigorous training programme his father had devised for him. This was not because he thought highly of Harrow – indeed he disparaged its teaching of mathematics as feeble – but because it was appropriate for a man of his social standing to send his sons to a leading public school. It was a rather heartless choice for Isambard, his elder son, who had a crippled leg and was bound to be exposed to much ragging. If Brunel was supposedly mortified when Isambard junior opted for the law, he should scarcely have been surprised.

At Duke Street Brunel created a special Shakespeare Room, adorned with pictures commissioned from eleven leading artists of the day. C. R. Leslie, friend and biographer of the painter John Constable, contributed scenes from *A Winter's Tale* and *Henry VIII*, Sir Edwin Landseer *Titania and Bottom*, for which he received a handsome 400 guineas. Meanwhile Brunel was already planning a princely pile to be built at Watcombe, 3 miles (5 km) north of Torquay, where he planned to retire and lord it over a garden of unique splendour. Between 1847 and his death in 1859 Brunel poured money into buying up land there, 136 acres (55 hectares) in all, and commissioned elaborate plans for the garden. His commitment to the place even drew him into local squabbles over a proposed gasworks. The great house, however, never got beyond foundation level.

Although the self-imposed pressure of work inevitably curtailed Brunel's social life, he numbered among his acquaintance the inventor Michael Faraday, Charles Babbage, creator of the proto-computer he styled a 'difference engine', and Edward Blore, consulting architect to Buckingham Palace and Westminster Abbey. The musical interests of Brunel's wife Mary brought him into contact with Felix Mendelssohn, the composer, a family friend of the Horsleys. Brunel's brother-in-law John Callcott Horsley was a Royal Academician. Another friend was the painter John Martin, whose depiction of the mouth of Hell in his illustrations for an edition of *Paradise Lost* was inspired by the Brunels' Thames Tunnel. Of his professional rivals, Robert Stephenson stood highest in Brunel's affection and respect. 'It is very delightful', he once wrote, 'in the midst of our incessant personal professional contests, carried to the extreme limit of fair opposition, to meet him on a perfectly friendly footing and discuss engineering points.'

Apart from discussing his profession with the only rival he considered his equal, Brunel was also prepared to hand down advice to budding aspirants, writing to one trainee engineer:

I must caution you strongly against studying *practical* mechanics among French authors – take them for abstract science and study their statics, dynamics, geometry etc. etc. to your heart's content but never even read any of their works on mechanics any more than you would search their modern authors for religious principles. A few hours spent in blacksmiths' and wheelwrights' shops will teach you more practical mechanics – read *English* books for practice – There is little enough to be learnt in them but you will not have to unlearn that little.

The Crimean War against Russia doubtless confirmed in Brunel, as in so many others who lived by their brains, a longstanding conviction of the incompetence of a military and naval establishment still dominated by aristocratic amateurs. Frustrated by news of the deadlock at the Russian fortress of Sebastopol, Brunel designed a floating siege-gun to be transported thither by means of a mother ship with opening bows. General Sir John Burgoyne, the leading military engineer of the day, took up the notion with enthusiasm but the Admiralty procrastinated successfully until Brunel gave up in disgust.

Another opportunity to contribute soon arose through Sir Benjamin Hawes, Brunel's brother-in-law, by then Permanent Under Secretary at the War Office. Stung by Florence Nightingale's well-publicised condemnations of the insanitary conditions in the military hospital at Scutari (Uskudar), Hawes invited Brunel to design a prefabricated hospital to supplement it. The formal request was made on 16th February 1855; by 5th March Brunel was mounting a presentation of the principles that have guided the layout of this type of temporary building ever since. It was a modular system, based on a standard unit of two wards, taking twenty-four patients each, complete with its own lavatories, nurses' rooms and outbuildings. Baths, wash-basins and ventilator fans were all included, together with a self-contained drainage system. By 12th July a hospital for three hundred had been erected by local labour under the direction of a gang of just eighteen skilled men sent out from England. By December it had a full quota of a thousand beds. Of the fifteen hundred men who passed through it only fifty died. To Brunel it was just an 'exercise of common sense'. At the Paris Exhibition of 1855 he was appointed to the Legion d'Honneur in recognition of his achievement. In 1857 his wide-ranging contribution to Britain, through public service as well as private enterprise, was indirectly recognised by the University of Oxford with the award of an honorary Doctorate of Civil Laws. In the same year Robert Stephenson stood down as President of the Institution of Civil Engineers and Brunel was pressed to succeed him. Deeply immersed in the greatest and final trial of his career, he declined the honour, already aware of the onset of what would prove a mortal illness.

The final trial

In the course of his work for the Great Exhibition Brunel had come into closer contact with John Scott Russell (1808–82), an early promoter of the venture and a fellow member of both the Royal Society and the Institution of Civil Engineers, whom he had known on and off since 1836. The two men were of an age and had been very similar in their youthful precocity. Russell, after studying at Edinburgh, St Andrews and Glasgow, had graduated at sixteen, served as acting professor of natural philosophy at twenty-four and through his experiments with wave motion had formulated fundamental principles of ship design which won him the gold medal of the Royal Society of Edinburgh at the age of twenty-nine. Nor was he any mere theorist. As manager of a shipyard he had built a fleet for the West India Royal Mail Company, designing four of the ships himself. He had also built a number of steam-powered road carriages. Moving to London in 1844, Russell had become Secretary of the Society of Arts the following year and thence moved into the inner group that dominated the planning and organisation of the Great Exhibition.

Russell was reputedly the most brilliant marine engineer of his day and it was to him that Brunel turned as a partner in the most ambitious venture he had yet envisaged – to build a steamship so immense it would be able, without refuelling, either to travel non-stop to Australia or to take a whole year's British exports to India,

returning laden with cotton and spices. At almost 700 feet (213 metres) in length it would be by far the largest ship ever built, five times bigger than anything attempted before. It would indeed be the largest built until the launching of the similarly ill-fated *Lusitania* in 1906. Attaining speeds of up to 14 knots, it would carry no less than four thousand passengers (ten thousand troops in case of national emergency), in

John Scott Russell (1808–82), Brunel's ill-chosen partner in the building of the 'Great Eastern'. The holly leaf seems oddly symbolic of their prickly relationship.

37

An early attempt to launch the 'Great Eastern'. Note the signal flag man beneath the paddle wheel and the presence of paying spectators.

addition to 6000 tons of cargo. Its construction would require the labours of up to two thousand men and boys. It would require over three million rivets and end up costing some £920,000. Brunel's modern biographer L. T. C. Rolt has hailed the building of what was initially known as *Leviathan* but subsequently became the *Great Eastern* as quite simply 'the most remarkable feat in the whole field of Victorian engineering ... the ultimate expression of ... boldness and daring ... the prototype of all subsequent ocean liners'.

Russell was soon fired with Brunel's enthusiasm and between them they used their many contacts to raise £120,000 initial capital. Thomas Brassey and Samuel Morton Peto, magnates of railway contracting, took a thousand shares apiece. Brunel took two thousand and, according to his own testimony, committed more of his time, thought and reputation to the enterprise than to anything he had ever done before. Russell's own yard at Millwall on the Isle of Dogs in east London was awarded the contract, despite the fact that his tender was both vague in details and substantially lower than Brunel's guesstimate of the probable costs. The actual construction site, Napier Yard, was linked to Russell's adjoining workshops by a special railway. Unforeseen problems, expenses and delays thrown up by making castings of unprecedented size and by Brunel's constant propensity to amend his specifications all lay in the troubled future. Meanwhile Brunel made his contribution to economy by designing the whole ship with only two gauges of plate and two sizes of angle iron. His contribution to naval architecture was to conceive the hull as a double-skin for extra strength and flotation.

Disagreements soured the relationship between Brunel and Russell almost as soon as the contract had been signed. The very method of payment became an immediate point of contention. Russell expected the shipbuilding industry's standard practice of lump sums at specified intervals. Brunel proposed 'railway style' monthly payments according to the amount of work done. Brunel won the point. In November 1854 an unsigned and in many details factually inaccurate article on 'Iron Steam Ships – the *Leviathan*' appeared in *The Observer* in which the anonymous author failed to credit Brunel with the concept of building a ship capable of sailing non-stop to Australia. It also implied that Brunel was merely a sort of supervisor while the true burden of design and construction fell on Russell. Brunel was furious, believing, almost certainly wrongly, that Russell was behind the article. When Prince Albert came to inspect the 'Great Ship' the following spring Russell went out of his way to stress Brunel's role as originator of the project, reassuring the engineer that 'I would much rather preserve your friendship than filch your fame..'. Brunel's many other commitments and distractions, compounded by his deteriorating health, reduced him virtually to nagging from the sidelines. Russell, for his part, was repeatedly disconcerted by Brunel's rejection (usually on grounds of cost) of his suggestions for building specialised equipment such as a dry dock, a mobile crane or hydraulic rams for the launching. Russell had, moreover, business distractions of his own. By September 1855 relations between the two men had sunk to the point where Brunel could reply to one of Russell's letters with the admonition 'I wish you were my obedient servant, I should begin with a little flogging'. Wrangles over payment continued. Brunel implied at one point that materials had gone missing, though stopped short of accusing Russell of outright peculation. Between February and May 1856 work came to a complete halt. In the autumn Russell took a diplomatic holiday and Brunel took charge in person, almost immediately prompting Yates, the yard manager, to protest at his high-handed management style: 'I feel strongly that, from your having failed in your attempt at a quarrel with Mr Russell, you appear determined to pick one with me.' It was in such a wretched atmosphere that the work of constructing the 12,000 ton hull was finally completed.

An initial launch deadline of October 1857 was missed. A first attempt was made on 3rd November. To his horror, Brunel found that the directors of the Eastern Steam Navigation Company had followed the example of their Thames Tunnel predecessors, sold three thousand tickets for the event and decked the yard out as

The 'Great Eastern' was finally launched on 31st January 1858 and in September 1859 underwent its first sea trials. Note how it dwarfs the ship alongside it.

though *en fête*. The total silence which had so signally marked the raising of the Saltash span but two months previously would be impossible in such chaotic circumstances, and the events of the day became a grotesque parody of the earlier disciplined exercise. In the event the bow section moved all of 3 feet (0.9 metre) and the stern 4 feet (1.2 metres). Disgruntled sightseers straggled home through the foggy damp consoled only by the awful death of an aged labourer whose legs had been smashed by a runaway winch. The addition of two more hydraulic rams made no difference at all when a second attempt was made on 19th November, but nine days later it shifted 14 feet (4.3 metres). After three further efforts moved it another 60 feet (18 metres) there was a delay of a month while a motley collection of thirty-six hydraulic presses and rams was assembled. Three further attempts were required before flotation was finally achieved on 31st January 1858. The men gave Brunel a spontaneous ovation but the strain and frustration had

Opposite page: Anxious eyes at the launching of the 'Great Eastern'; from left to right, John Scott Russell, Henry Wakefield, Brunel and Solomon Tredwell.

Below: The huge baulks of timber supports remain in situ at the 'Great Eastern' launch site.

The 'Great Eastern' towed to her moorings off Deptford. An engraving from the 'Illustrated London News', 6th February 1858.

broken him to the point of exhaustion and the expense had driven the company into bankruptcy.

Between May and September Brunel took what was in theory a convalescent tour, though in fact he continued to work on designs for the Eastern Bengal Railway. Returning briefly for the sale of the uncompleted ship to a new ' Great Ship Company ' and to prepare specifications for its fitting out, Brunel left again for warmer shores on medical advice as he had now been definitely diagnosed as suffering from nephritis, a kidney disease. On Christmas Day he dined in Cairo with his old friend Robert Stephenson. When he finally returned to England in May 1859 he found to his astonishment that the new owners of 'his' ship had awarded the fitting-out contract to Russell. Undeterred, Brunel spent his last strength preparing for the sea trials of the ship. The severity of his illness, however, cheated him of even seeing it depart under steam. On 5th September he was cut down by a stroke and carried from the ship for the last time. Three days later she lay at the Nore and Brunel had recovered enough to be dictating letters and instructions.

The *Great Eastern* at last steamed majestically past the Nore Light at 13 knots on the morning of 9th September. Meanwhile, below

The statue of Brunel in Bristol.

decks, disaster lay in wait. Temporary stopcocks on the water-jackets of the leading and second funnels had been overlooked at the last moment and left closed. Mercifully the saloon was deserted when the explosion occurred at 6.05 a.m. but men in the boiler room were hideously scalded. Up above, the *Times* correspondent saw the forward deck blow like a mine as a funnel rose into the air and steam gushed forth to shroud a deadly cascade of 'glass, giltwork, saloon ornaments and pieces of wood'. Brunel's cellular construction, however, effectively confined the force of the explosion to the grand saloon and not one passenger was harmed. In the library adjoining not a mirror was cracked, not a book out of place. But for Brunel himself it was fate's last cruel stroke. He had no strength to rally with and died on 15th September 1859.

Daniel Gooch, one of Brunel's closest colleagues, observed:

> By his death the greatest of England's engineers was lost, the man with the greatest originality of thought and power of execution, bold in his plans but right. The commercial world thought him extravagant; but although he was so, things are not done by those who sit down and count the cost of every thought and act.

Brunel never did.

43

Envoi

Robert Stephenson died, also of nephritis, a month after Brunel. Daniel Gooch went on to use the *Great Eastern* to lay the first Atlantic cable and become a Member of Parliament and a baronet. The *Great Eastern* went on to lay a further three Atlantic cables and another from Aden to Bombay but never fulfilled the purposes envisioned by Brunel. After a working life of just sixteen years, it was beached for eleven years at Milford Haven – another Brunel dock – and was finally broken up ignominiously at Birkenhead in 1891. John Scott Russell went on to design the Royal Navy's first ironclad, HMS *Warrior*, to found the Institution of Naval Architects and to write the first standard multi-volume authority on naval architecture; but the *Dictionary of National Biography*, while praising his 'brilliant and versatile intellectual powers', also noted that 'a certain lack of stability, or of the business capacity so rarely united to inventive genius, hampered his success in life'. Brunel's elder son, Isambard, eventually became Chancellor of the Diocese of Ely, while his younger, Henry Marc, did become an engineer. His daughter, Florence Mary, married a master at Eton College.

A memorial window to Brunel was erected in Westminster Abbey in 1868. A committee chaired by Lord Shelburne commissioned Baron Carlo Marochetti to make bronze statues of both Robert Stephenson and Brunel. The list of subscribers to Brunel's memorial ranged from the contracting magnate Sir Samuel Morton Peto, who forwarded the maximum £10, to Mr R. Rowse and five fellow Cornish railwaymen, who sent 2s 3d. Originally it was intended that the

statue should stand in Parliament Square, near the corner of Great George Street, where the Institution of Civil Engineers had its offices, but it was not until 1877 that a site was finally found at Temple Place, where Brunel now thoughtfully gazes towards the piers which are all that remains of his Hungerford Suspension Bridge (built 1841–5), the chains having been recycled to be used at Clifton – an uncharacteristically economic epitaph for a life of extravagance.

The Brunel memorial, by Baron Marochetti, at the corner of Temple Place, London WC2.

Principal events

1806   Brunel is born at Portsea, Portsmouth, on 9th April.
1818   Institution of Civil Engineers founded.
1820   Brunel goes to Caen.
1821   Marc Brunel imprisoned for debt.
1822   Brunel leaves Lycée Henri Quatre and goes to work for his father.
1825   Work begins on the Thames Tunnel. Stockton & Darlington Railway opened.
1827   Thames Tunnel flooded.
1828   Thames Tunnel abandoned.
1830   Brunel wins Clifton Bridge competition. Liverpool & Manchester Railway opened. Brunel enrols as a special constable during the Bristol riots. Brunel elected a Fellow of the Royal Society.
1832   First Reform Bill passed.
1833   Brunel appointed Engineer to the Great Western Railway.
1835   Brunel proposes to build a steamship for a Bristol – New York service.
1836   Brunel marries Mary Horsley. Foundation stone of Clifton Bridge laid.
1837   Accession of Queen Victoria. Hull of the *Great Western* launched.
1838   First section of the Great Western Railway, from Paddington to Maidenhead, is opened. *Great Western* crosses the Atlantic.
1839   Construction of *Great Britain* begins.
1841   Great Western Railway opened (London to Bristol).
1842   Queen Victoria travels by train for the first time on the Great Western Railway.
1843   Swindon locomotive works opened. Thames Tunnel opened. *Great Britain* launched.
1845   Maiden voyage of the *Great Britain*.
1846   *Great Britain* runs aground at Dundrum Day, County Down.
1847   Atmospheric railway runs in Devon. Institution of Mechanical Engineers founded.
1848   Brunel enrols as a special constable.
1849   South Devon Railway completed. Windsor branch of GWR opened. Death of Sir Marc Brunel.
1850   West Cornwall Railway opened.
1851   Great Exhibition.
1854   Paddington New Station opened. Crimean War begins. Royal Albert Bridge over river Tamar begun.
1855   Brunel designs prefabricated hospital for the Crimea.
1856   Crimean War ends.
1857   *Great Western* broken up at Vauxhall. Brunel honoured by Oxford University.
1858   *Great Eastern* launched.
1859   Royal Albert Bridge completed. Maiden voyage of the *Great Eastern*. Brunel dies on 15th September.
1860   Institution of Naval Architects founded.
1862   Richard Beamish FRS publishes *Memoir of the Life of Sir Marc Isambard Brunel*.
1864   Clifton Suspension Bridge opened.
1870   Isambard Brunel publishes *The Life of Isambard Kingdom Brunel – Civil Engineer*.
1877   Statue of Brunel by Baron Carlo Marochetti unveiled at Temple Place.

Further reading

Ball, Adrian, and Wright, Diana. *SS Great Britain*. David & Charles, 1981.
Beckett, Derrick. *Brunel's Britain*. David & Charles, 1980.
Buchanan, R.A. *The Engineers: A History of the Engineering Profession in Britain 1750–1914*. Jessica Kingsley Publishers, 1989.
Buchanan, R.A., and Williams, M. *Brunel's Bristol*. Redcliffe Press, 1982.
Buck, Alan. *The Little Giant: A Life of I. K. Brunel*. David & Charles, 1986.
Burton, Anthony. *The Railway Builders*. John Murray, 1992.
Clements, Paul. *Marc Isambard Brunel*. Longman, 1970.
Hay, Peter. *Brunel: His Achievements in the Transport Revolution*. Osprey, 1973.
Pudney, John. *Brunel and His World*. Thames & Hudson, 1974.
Pugsley, Sir Alfred (editor). *The Works of Isambard Kingdom Brunel: An Engineering Appreciation*. Cambridge University Press, 1980.
Rolt, L.T.C. *Isambard Kingdom Brunel*. Longman, 1957; Penguin, 1975.
Rolt, L.T.C. *Victorian Engineering*. Penguin, 1970.
Simmons, J. (editor). *The Birth of the Great Western Railway: Extracts from the Diary and Correspondence of George Henry Gibbs*. Adams & Dart, 1971.
Vaughan, Adrian. *Isambard Kingdom Brunel: Engineering Knight Errant*. John Murray, 1991.

The main collection of Brunel manuscripts and documentation is held at the University of Bristol library (http://www.bris.ac.uk/Depts/Library/brunel.htm).

At last to rest – the Brunel family grave at Kensal Green Cemetery, London. At the time of Brunel's death the traffic of the Great Western Railway a few hundred yards away would still have been audible.

Seeing Brunel's work

London

Seventeenth-century Lindsey House, Brunel's home from 1811 to 1826, still stands, though now numbered 98 Cheyne Row (then known as 4 Lindsey Row). Statues of Brunel are to be seen at Paddington station (beside platform 1) and on the Embankment at Temple Place. The Brunel family grave is in Kensal Green Cemetery, about halfway between the southern entrance and the main chapel on the left-hand side, 10 feet (3 metres) or so off the main path. There is a memorial window to Brunel in the nave of Westminster Abbey. The Science Museum (Exhibition Road, South Kensington, London SW7 2DD; telephone: 020 7942 4000; website: www.nmsi.ac.uk) has models of the Portsmouth block-making machinery, the Thames Tunnel, the *Great Western*, *Great Britain* and *Great Eastern*. The National Maritime Museum (Romney Road, Greenwich, London SE10 9NF; telephone: 020 8858 4422; website: www.nmm.ac.uk) has a model of the *Great Britain* and William Parnatt's painting *Building the Great Eastern*. The launch site of the *Great Eastern* is still visible at Millwall on the Isle of Dogs. The restored Thames Tunnel engine-house is at Rotherhithe. It is claimed that the Engineer public house at Gloucester Avenue, Primrose Hill, was designed by Brunel in 1841.

The route of the Great Western Railway

Visibly surviving features include the Wharncliffe Viaduct at Hanwell, 7 miles (11 km) west of Paddington; the wrought-iron Thames bridge on the Slough–Windsor spur; the brick bridges at Maidenhead, Basildon (Berkshire) and Moulsford; Sonning Cutting; stations at Mortimer and Culham; the viaducts at Chippenham and Bath; and the west portal of Box Tunnel. Brunel's Tunnel House Hotel at Saltford claims that it was formerly lived in by Brunel. The Great Western Society (established 1964) has amassed a collection of twenty locomotives and forty examples of rolling-stock at the Didcot Railway Centre, Didcot, Oxfordshire OX11 7NJ (telephone: 01235 817200; website: www.didcotrailwaycentre.org.uk). Steam – Museum of the Great Western Railway, Kemble Drive, Swindon, Wiltshire SN2 2TA; telephone: 01793 466646; website: www.swindonweb.com/steam) has a Brunel display which includes not only photographs and documents but also his drawing-board and other tools of his trade.

In Bristol, apart from Temple Meads station and the Clifton Suspension Bridge and its excellent visitor centre (www.clifton-suspension-bridge.org.uk), there is also the brilliantly restored SS *Great Britain* (www.SS-great-britain.com) in Great Western Dock. *Bertha*, a dredger probably designed by Brunel in 1844 and now the world's oldest working steamboat, was built in Bristol. A statue of Brunel stands just off Broad Quay at Marsh Street.

The Royal Albert Bridge still spans the Tamar at Saltash, Cornwall. A pumping house for the atmospheric railway can be seen at Starcross in Devon.

A bronze statue of Brunel stands on the site of the old station at Neyland, Pembrokeshire, terminus of Brunel's main line through South Wales.

Index

Page numbers in italic refer to illustrations.